Dragon at the Pool

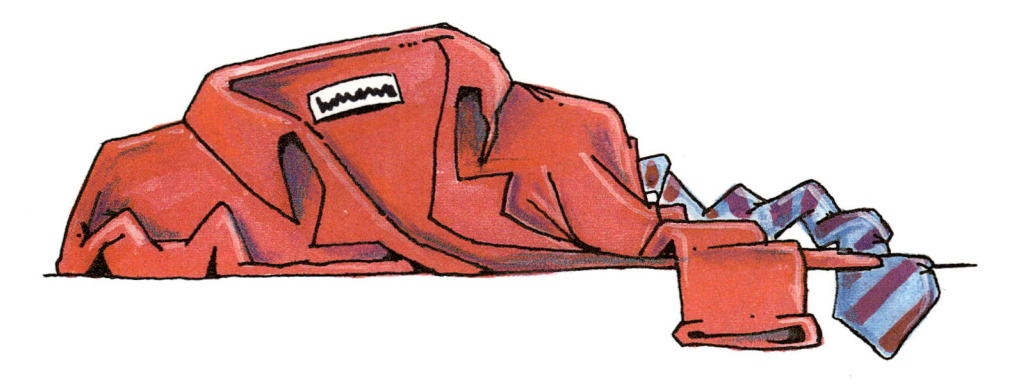

Written by Susheila Stone
Illustrated by Rob Englebright

Collins Educational
An imprint of HarperCollins*Publishers*

Dragon took off his hat.

He took off his shirt.

He took off his trousers.

He put on his trunks.

He put on his goggles.

He jumped in the pool.

He put out his fire!